SOCCER GOAL SUFFIXES

By Michael Ruscoe
Cover illustrated by Scott Angle
Interior illustrated by Jeff Chandler
Language arts curriculum consultant: Debra Voege, M.A.

Gareth Stevens
Publishing

Please visit our web site at **www.garethstevens.com**.
For a free color catalog describing Gareth Stevens Publishing's list of
high-quality books, call 1-800-542-2595 (USA) or 1-800-387-3178 (Canada).
Gareth Stevens Publishing's fax: 1-877-542-2596

Library of Congress Cataloging-in-Publication Data

Ruscoe, Michael.
   Soccer goal suffixes / by Michael Ruscoe ; illustrated by Jeff Chandler ;
language arts curriculum consultant: Debra Voege, M.A.
     p. cm. — (Grammar all-stars: kinds of words)
    At head of title : Grammar all-stars : kinds of words
     ISBN-10: 1-4339-0012-2 ISBN-13: 978-1-4339-0012-9 (lib. bdg.)
     ISBN-10: 1-4339-0154-4 ISBN-13: 978-1-4339-0154-6 (pbk.)
     1. English language—Suffixes and prefixes—Juvenile literature.
  2. English language—Word formation—Juvenile literature. 3. English
language—Grammar—Juvenile literature. I. Voege, Debra. II. Title.
III. Title: Grammar all-stars : kinds of words.
PE1175.R88 2008
428—dc22   2008030379

This edition first published in 2009 by
Gareth Stevens Publishing
A Weekly Reader® Company
1 Reader's Digest Road
Pleasantville, NY 10570-7000 USA

Executive Managing Editor: Lisa M. Herrington
Senior Editor: Barbara Bakowski
Creative Director: Lisa Donovan
Art Director: Ken Crossland
Publisher: Keith Garton

Printed in the United States of America

1 2 3 4 5 6 7 8 9 10 09 08

CONTENTS

Look for the **boldface** words on each page.
Then read the **SOCCER KICK CLUE** that follows.

CHAPTER 1

THE CHAMPIONSHIP KICKS OFF

What Are Suffixes?

"Hello, **viewers**! I'm Buzz Star for P-L-A-Y TV. Welcome to the Swift Kick Soccer **Championship**. Today's match is between the first-place Terrytown Titans and the hometown Cap City Cyclones." Buzz turns to a boy in the broadcast booth. "**Calling** the action with me is kid **reporter** Eddie Finale. Say hello to the folks at home, Eddie!"

"Hi, everyone," Eddie says. "It's **wonderful** to be here."

"Tell everyone how you **landed** your job in the booth today, Eddie," says Buzz.

"I got straight A's and won the Reach Your Goal contest at school," Eddie says.

"Wow, straight A's!" says Buzz. "You must be one of the **smartest** kids in your class."

REPORT CARD

English....A+

Math.......A

Science...A

story.....A

Gym........A

"I had the best grade in English," says Eddie **proudly**. "We **learned** all about suffixes."

"Suffixes?" says Buzz. "That must have been hard!"

"No, it was **easy**," Eddie replies. "It was **simpler** than you would think! A suffix is just a letter or group of letters **added** to the end of a base word."

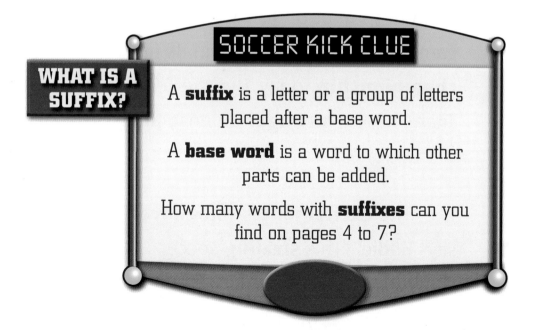

SOCCER KICK CLUE

WHAT IS A SUFFIX?

A **suffix** is a letter or a group of letters placed after a base word.

A **base word** is a word to which other parts can be added.

How many words with **suffixes** can you find on pages 4 to 7?

"**Needless** to say, I am **certainly** glad you won the contest!" Buzz exclaims. "Are you **having** fun as a kid **reporter**?"

"Oh, yes!" Eddie says. "I feel **lucky** to help you cover this game. I've met a lot of **players** on both teams. The **greatest** moment was when I met Cyclones **striker** Kick Malloy."

"Kick is the most **famous** star on the field today," Buzz says. "He is **skillful** and brings a lot of **quickness** to the game. Cap City hopes to win its first **championship** today. But the Terrytown Titans have a **stronger** defense than the Cyclones."

"The **excitement** is **unbelievable**," says Eddie. "This **sizzling** soccer showdown is about to kick off!"

COMMON SUFFIXES

Some common suffixes are **-ed**, **-ing**, **-est**, **-ness**, **-less**, **-able**, **-ly**, **-ful**, **-ment**, **-ship**, **-ous**, and **-y**.

Adding a suffix to a base word **changes its meaning**.

Examples: great**est** = most great
need**less** = not needed
skill**ful** = having skill

Adding a suffix sometimes **changes the part of speech**.

Examples: view = to look (**verb**)
view**er** = one who looks (**noun**)

proud = pleased (**adjective**)
proud**ly** = in a proud way (**adverb**)

Some suffixes, such as **-er**, have **more than one meaning**.

Example: report + **er** = report**er** (one who reports)

strong + **er** = strong**er** (more strong)

CHAPTER 2

S-C-O-R-E!

Spelling With Suffixes

"The match is underway, soccer fans!"
says Buzz. "The two captains walked
onto the field for the coin toss. Cyclones
captain Kick Malloy made his call as the
referee **flipped** the coin into the air. After
winning the toss, the Cyclones kicked off."

Eddie takes over. "So far, the Cyclones
have **controlled** the action. Kick is
running up and down the field, **cutting**
from side to side. Although the Titans
are **bigger**, Kick has **stunned** them
with his speed."

"There is no score yet," Buzz adds. "The two goalkeepers have **stopped** every shot. But now Kick is turning upfield near the center circle. He has **slipped** past the Titans defense and picked up a loose ball. He fires a pass to teammate Flick Fussball. Flick's header **whizzed** just past the goalie! The Cyclones have **netted** a goal!"

SOCCER KICK CLUE

Sometimes, adding a suffix to a base word **changes the spelling** of the base word.

For most one-syllable base words that **end in a single consonant**, **double the last letter** when adding a suffix.

If a base word **ends with more than one consonant**, **do not double** the last letter.

"The hometown team gets on the board by **scoring** first!" Eddie says. "The crowd is **noisy** now, Buzz."

Buzz picks up the action. "The players are **battling**. Titans forward Pitch Peters is **dribbling** the ball. He's **weaving** left and right. He passes to Arch Anderson."

"The Cyclones are **hoping** to keep the lead," Eddie says. "But they are **having** some trouble, Buzz. They seem to be **tiring**."

He Shoots,
He Scores!

"I agree," Buzz adds. "Anderson is **driving** down the field. He's **racing** past the Cyclones sweeper. He shoots. Cyclones goalie Ken Keeper is **diving** to make the save. But the ball gets past him! The score is tied at one goal apiece."

"That is bad news for Cyclones fans," says Eddie.

"Kick Malloy has the ball once again," Buzz continues. "He is **fading** left, **confusing** the Titans defenders. He gets ready to kick. Look out! A Terrytown player fouls him from behind! Turf Tooruff was **sliding** into the Cyclones star!"

"The referee is **giving** Tooruff a yellow card," says Eddie. "Another foul and he'll be out of the game."

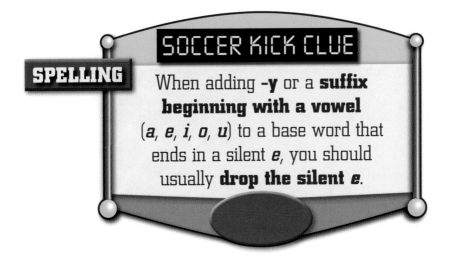

SPELLING

SOCCER KICK CLUE

When adding **-y** or a **suffix beginning with a vowel** (*a, e, i, o, u*) to a base word that ends in a silent *e*, you should usually **drop the silent e**.

"The Cyclones are **hurrying** back up the field," Buzz says. "Storm Winz **tried** to center a pass to Kick Malloy, but the ball was blocked. That's a turnover."

Eddie frowns. "Winz could have been **luckier** on that play."

"A Titans winger has **carried** the ball upfield," says Buzz. "Cap City is **trying** to get it back."

"Flick Fussball is the **speediest** player on the field," Eddie says. "He steals the ball! The Cyclones fans are cheering **noisily**."

"Flick makes a **beautiful** pass to Kick Malloy," says Buzz. "Wow! Kick has **buried** a header in the net!"

"It's the winning goal for the Cyclones!" Eddie shouts. "Kick must be the **happiest** player on the field."

"What a match! Stay tuned for our postgame coverage," Buzz says.

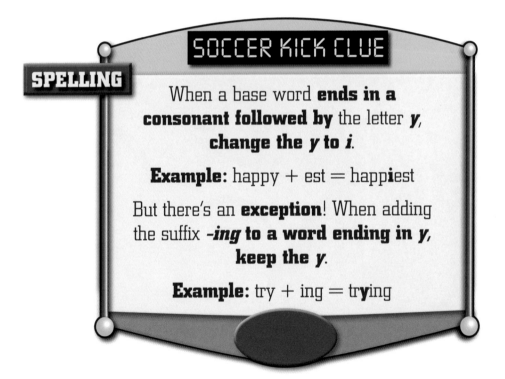

SPELLING

SOCCER KICK CLUE

When a base word **ends in a consonant followed by** the letter *y*, **change the *y* to *i*.**

Example: happy + est = happiest

But there's an **exception**! When adding the suffix *-ing* to a word ending in *y*, **keep the *y*.**

Example: try + ing = trying

CHAPTER 3

POSTGAME WRAP-UP

Building Words With Suffixes

"Welcome back, viewers," Buzz says after the break. "P-L-A-Y TV kid reporter Eddie Finale is in the Cyclones' locker room. Take it away, Eddie!"

"Thanks, Buzz," says Eddie. "I'm here with today's hero, Kick Malloy. Kick, the score was tied late in the game. Overtime seemed **unavoidable**. What were you thinking then?"

"Honestly, Eddie, I was **uncomfortable**," Kick says. "The Titans defense was **unbeatable**!"

"Tell us about the foul by Turf Tooruff."

"I was tackled **illegally**," Kick replies. "And when Tooruff got a yellow card, he became **disagreeable**!"

SUFFIXES PLUS PREFIXES

SOCCER KICK CLUE

A **prefix** is a letter or group of letters placed before a base word. You can add a suffix to a word that has a prefix.

Example: unbeat**able**

"Time was running out. There was a feeling of **helplessness** on the bench. You are the team captain. What did you say to your players?" Eddie asks.

"I looked **nervously** into the stands," Kick says. "I could see the fans cheering **hopefully**. I told the team we couldn't let our fans down. **Thankfully**, we didn't," Kick adds **cheerfully**.

SOCCER KICK CLUE

MULTIPLE SUFFIXES

You can add **more than one suffix** to a single base word.

Example: help + **less** + **ness** = helplessness

"Your fans want to know, Kick," Eddie says. "What does the future hold for you?"

"**Retirement**," says Kick. "I know your **viewers** will be **surprised**. Today was the **greatest** game of my career. I'd like to go out **proudly**!"

"This **championship** is a **memorable** finish," Eddie says. There is **sadness** in his voice. "Soccer fans are **thankful** for the **enjoyment** you gave us. Now back to you, Buzz!"

"Thanks, Eddie," says Buzz. "You did a **wonderful** job today! I hope you had fun as my kid **reporter**."

"I **certainly** did, Buzz," says Eddie **happily**. "It was a real kick!"

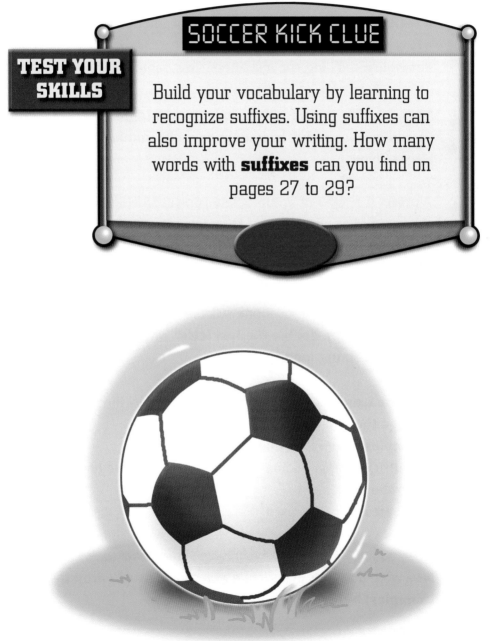

SOCCER KICK CLUE

TEST YOUR SKILLS

Build your vocabulary by learning to recognize suffixes. Using suffixes can also improve your writing. How many words with **suffixes** can you find on pages 27 to 29?

A **base word** is a word to which other letters or word parts can be added.
Examples: wonder, happy, friend, run, fast, big, shine

A **suffix** is a letter or group of letters placed at the end of a base word.
Examples: -ed, -ing, -er, -est, -ness, -less, -able, -ly, -ful, -y

Adding a suffix changes a base word's **meaning**.
Examples: wonder**ful**, happi**ness**, friend**ly**, runn**ing**, fast**est**, bigg**er**, shin**y**

A **prefix** is a letter or group of letters placed before a base word. You can add a suffix to a word that has a prefix.
Examples: unfriend**ly**, **im**perfect**ly**

Adding a suffix to a base word may change the **spelling** of the new word. For most one-syllable base words that end in a single consonant, **double the last letter** when adding a suffix.
Examples: sun**n**y, jo**gg**ing

If a base word ends in a consonant followed by the letter *y*, **change the *y* to *i*.**
Examples: happ**i**er, funn**i**est
EXCEPTION: When adding the suffix –*ing* to a word ending in *y*, **keep the *y*.**
Examples: hurr**y**ing, tr**y**ing

When adding –*y* or a suffix beginning with a vowel (*a, e, i, o, u*) to a base word that ends in a silent *e*, you should usually **drop the silent e**.
Examples: hik**ing**, nois**y**

Eddie Finale wrote a thank-you letter to Cylones star Kick Malloy.

On a piece of paper, **list the words with suffixes**.

Dear Mr. Malloy,

Recently, I was lucky to be a kid reporter at the Swift Kick Soccer Championship. At first, I was nervous. I was not comfortable on TV. But the action was thrilling!

Before the game, I carefully read the rules. I studied up on the famous players. But I learned the most by watching you. You never gave up, even when things were hopeless. You taught me a valuable lesson. Skillfulness takes commitment. I know I can reach my goals—if I try my hardest.

Sincerely,
Eddie Finale

All-Star Challenge

For each word on your list, write the **base word**.
(Spelling counts!)

Turn the page to check your answers and to see how many points you scored!

31

ANSWER KEY

Did you score enough suffixes to be a soccer superstar?

0–5 words with suffixes: Red Card!   **11–15** words with suffixes: Nice Pass!

6–10 words with suffixes: Yellow Card!   **16–20** words with suffixes: GOAL!

WORDS WITH SUFFIXES

1. Recently
2. lucky
3. reporter
4. Championship
5. nervous
6. comfortable
7. action
8. thrilling
9. carefully
10. studied
11. famous
12. players
13. learned
14. watching
15. hopeless
16. valuable
17. Skillfulness
18. commitment
19. hardest
20. Sincerely

All-Star Challenge

1. Recent
2. luck
3. report
4. Champion
5. nerve
6. comfort
7. act
8. thrill
9. care
10. study
11. fame
12. play
13. learn
14. watch
15. hope
16. value
17. Skill
18. commit
19. hard
20. Sincere